GYMNASTICS
THE VAULT

JOANNE MATTERN

The Rourke Corporation, Inc.
Vero Beach, Florida 32964

PROJECT EDITOR:
Genger Thorn is a professional member of USA and AAU gymnastics associations. She is USA safety certified and an associate member of the US Elite Coaches Association (USECA). Genger is currently a girls team coach and director at East Coast Gymnastics, Merritt Island, Florida.

PHOTO CREDITS:
All photos Tony Gray

EDITORIAL SERVICES:
Janice L. Smith for Penworthy Learning Systems

Library of Congress Cataloging-in-Publication Data

Mattern, Joanne, 1963-
  Gymnastics / by Joanne Mattern
     p. cm.
  Includes bibliographical references and indexes.
  Contents: [1] Training and fitness — [2] The pommel horse and the rings —
[3] The vault — [4] Balance beam and floor exercises — [5] Uneven parallel bars —
[6] Parallel bars and horizontal bar.
  ISBN 0-86593-571-8 (v.1). — ISBN 0-86593-568-8 (v. 2). — ISBN 0-86593-566-1
(v. 3). — ISBN 0-86593-567.X (v. 4). — ISBN 0-86593-569-6 (v. 5). — ISBN 0-86593-
570-X (v. 6)
  1. Gymnastics for children Juvenile literature. [1. Gymnastics.] I. Title
GV464.5.M38 1999
796.44—dc21   99-27924
                                                                        CIP

Printed in the USA

TABLE OF CONTENTS

WOMEN'S VAULT

5 feet 4 inches (1.6 m)

Springboard

MEN'S VAULT

14 inches (36 cm)

Springboard

CHAPTER ONE

A UNIQUE EVENT

A gymnastics meet consists of many different events. But the vaulting event is unique. Vaulting is the only event that does not require the gymnast to perform a **routine** (roo TEEN), or a series of moves. Instead, a vault shows off a single skill.

In vaulting, a gymnast runs toward a vaulting **horse** (HAWRS) at top speed. When the gymnast reaches the horse, he or she jumps up and flies over the horse. His or her body extends fully and becomes tight as the gymnast **blocks** (BLAHKS), or pushes off, the horse high into the air. Then he or she lands in front of the horse. Vaults are judged on height, distance, body position, landing, and degree of difficulty. The entire event lasts only a few seconds.

Vaulting has been part of gymnastics competitions since the late 1820s. It is one of the most popular gymnastic events. Gymnasts enjoy the high-speed run up to the horse. They also enjoy flying through the air. And spectators enjoy watching these exciting actions!

Differences Between Men and Women

Both men and women compete in the vault. However, they never compete against each other. Men compete against men, and women compete against women.

Springboards are placed in front of the horse to give gymnasts greater height in their takeoffs.

Both men and women compete in the vault, but in different ways. The horse used in women's vaulting is no taller than 47-1/4 inches (120 cm), and it is 64 inches (160 cm) long. The height can be lowered for smaller gymnasts. Women can run up to 79 feet (24 m) to approach the horse. A woman gets two chances to vault, but only the higher score counts.

The horse used in men's vaulting is higher, since most male gymnasts are taller than female gymnasts. A men's horse can be as tall as 53 inches (135 cm), although it can be lowered for shorter gymnasts. A man's run up to the vault can be no more than 65 feet, 7 inches (20 m). Men get only one vault attempt.

The biggest difference between men's and women's vaulting is the position of the horse. For women, the horse is placed sideways. This means that women jump across the width of the horse. At advanced levels the horse is turned 90 degrees for the men's events. Vaulting across the length of the horse showcases a man's great physical strength.

THE EQUIPMENT

The Horse

   The vaulting and **pommel** (PAHM ul) horse events used
to take place on the same horse. The only difference was
that in vaulting the pommels, or handles, were removed.
Today, for safety reasons most gyms no longer use the
same horse for both events.

The horse has a long and interesting history. In the 1700s, riders in Europe used a wooden horse to practice stunts such as standing on their head in the saddle. Once they had mastered these stunts on the wooden horse, they tried them on an actual galloping horse. The original wooden horse was about five feet (152 cm) high and had legs, a head, and even a tail! Leather straps were placed on the horse's back to mark where a saddle would be on a real horse.

In the 1800s, a man named Friedrich Jahn trained on the wooden horse while in the German army. Later, Jahn became a gymnastics teacher. He invented several gymnastics events and was responsible for developing gymnastics as part of the European educational system. Because of his contributions to the sport, Jahn is considered the father of modern gymnastics.

Jahn thought that his students could do some exercises on the horse. Jahn streamlined the horse and replaced the saddle straps with two curved handles called pommels.

Today, horses are made from a combination of wood and steel. They are wrapped with soft padding and covered with leather or a synthetic material. This covering is specially designed to prevent the gymnast from slipping.

Don't try any new moves before practicing them with your coach first.

The Springboard

A **springboard** (SPRING bawrd) is placed in front of the horse to help the gymnast achieve a strong, high jump. The springboard is also called a beatboard, or a Reuther board after the man who invented it. A springboard is about 4 feet (1.2 meters) long, 3 feet (1 meter) wide, and 5 inches (12-1/2 centimeters) high. The board is covered with a nonskid, carpet material. Beneath the board is a coiled spring that pushes the gymnast into the air.

Gymnasts place the springboard at a comfortable distance from the horse. This distance is determined by the type of vault the gymnast is trying to do, and by his or her size and ability level.

Mats

A thick **mat** (MAT) is placed on the far side of the horse to provide a soft, safe landing for the gymnast. A thinner mat (about 3/4-inch or 2 centimeters thick) is also placed on the runway to give the gymnast a safe surface to run on and protect him or her in case of a fall.

APPROACH
AND TAKEOFF

The **approach** (uh PROCH), or run, is the key to a successful vault. A gymnast must run fast with long, even strides to gain enough momentum to hit the springboard strongly and perform a successful vault. In general, a faster run leads to a better vault. Many gymnastics coaches even bring in track-and-field coaches to help gymnasts improve their running techniques.

The approach to the springboard should start with two or three trotting steps. Your speed should build steadily, until you are running at just under full speed as you near the springboard. The final three or four steps before the board should be as fast as possible.

You should develop your own running technique, keeping several guidelines in mind. In general, your feet should point straight forward. Lift your knees high to maximize the driving force from your legs. Your stride should lengthen as your speed increases.

As you run, your arms should swing back and forth with a bend at the elbow. These arm movements help keep you balanced and work with your legs to maintain a steady rhythm. Your arms should never swing in front of your chest—they should remain at the sides of your body. Keep your eyes focused straight ahead on both the springboard and the horse. As you near the end of your run, focus on the horse as you plan where to place your body.

An approach to the springboard

Land on the springboard with both feet to get enough height for a
successful vault.

It's important for you to learn how much distance you need to cover in your approach to the vault. Some gymnasts need a longer run to build up speed. Others can achieve top speed in fewer steps. Experiment with several distances to discover what is most comfortable. Once you find the right distance, try to make all of your approaches exactly the same. For example, you should take the same number of steps for each approach. The length of your stride should remain constant, and your speed should increase at the same rate each time. Making your approaches consistent will help your vaults become more consistent, too.

The Final Step

The final step of the approach is called the **hurdle** (HER dl). It starts as a leap that drives your front foot off the floor to complete a long jump onto the board. Your trailing foot should come forward at the same time so that both feet are together when you land on the springboard. You must land on the springboard with both feet to get enough height to perform a successful vault.

★ COACH'S CORNER

Practicing Your Approach

Place a springboard in front of a mat. Run to the board and take off with both feet, just as you would during a vault. Pretend you are jumping over an obstacle and land on the pad. After you've practiced this a few times, place a low bench or rolled-up mat between the springboard and the mat and practice jumping over it.

It is important that your run flows smoothly into the hurdle. You don't want to stop and then hop onto the board. Running smoothly into the hurdle allows all the forward movement of your body to be changed into rising movement as you spring off the board. This gives your **takeoff** (TAYK AWF) greater height and creates a more successful vault.

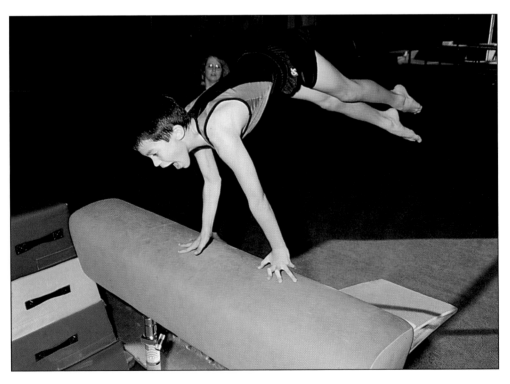

Your hands are the only part of your body that should touch the vault.

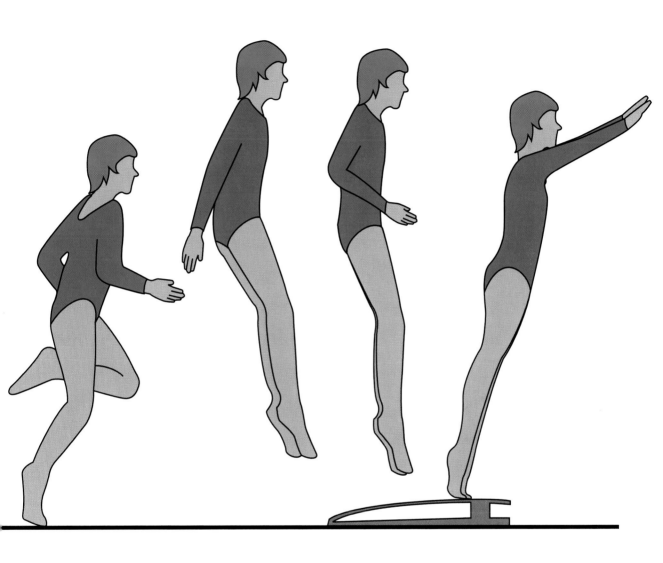

The proper approach to jumping onto a springboard

Takeoff

Your takeoff lifts you into flight over the horse. For a good takeoff, your hurdle should land just behind the highest point of the springboard. This is the place where the board has the most spring.

Land on the balls of your feet. As you land, bend your knees, hips, and ankles slightly. Then straighten them quickly to thrust yourself up into the air.

Your arms will also help you move upward. Just before you step into the hurdle, swing your arms back and down. After you hit the springboard, your movements will vary depending on what type of vault you are performing. For a squat vault swing up and forward about to your shoulders. Swing your arms higher, about to your ears, for more advanced vaults.

The way your body is leaning as you hit the springboard will determine the height of your takeoff. Leaning forward creates a low flight. It is better to keep your body vertical or to lean slightly backward. These positions help your body fly higher.

★ COACH'S CORNER

Building Confidence

It is important to learn how to take off and land safely before you perform an actual vault. Practice running up to the springboard. Concentrate on where your arms and legs are positioned and how they are moving. You might want to practice jumping off the springboard onto a box or other raised surface until you feel you can take off and land with confidence.

CONTACT!

   Your flight to the horse after takeoff is called **preflight** (PREE FLIT). You should move through the air with your body extended and your arms held straight over your head. Make sure your hands are open with the palms down and ready for contact with the horse. You don't want to skim over the top of the horse. You want to push off solidly from the horse and get as much height as you can.

As you become more experienced at vaulting, you will learn exactly how high and far you need to travel to reach the horse from the springboard. Distance and height can be changed by varying your body position and placement of the springboard. Certain types of vaults require a higher preflight, while other vaults work better with a lower preflight. You will learn these things as you do more vaults. At first, it's best to concentrate on achieving good height and keeping your body extended.

Hands Down!

Your hands are the only part of your body to touch the horse. Your hands have only one job—to get off quickly. Along with the extension of your entire body, your hands push you up and away from the horse. This is called **repulsion** (reh PUL shun). The tighter your body and the straighter the extension, the higher you will go. Your hands must **pivot** (PIV ut), or turn, your body to move it into the vault.

★ COACH'S CORNER

Hand Contact Exercises

There are several ways you can work on your hand contact without actually vaulting. One way is to stand on a mat and dive forward onto your hands. As soon as your hands touch the floor, push yourself back to a standing position.

Proper hand position is important for a good launch off the vault.

The position of this gymnast's hands is perfect for performing a squat vault.

As you prepare for contact with the horse, your hands should be flat and shoulder-width apart. Your arms should be straight and your palms open. Your entire hand should touch the horse.

Afterflight

The movement from repulsion to landing is called the **afterflight** (AF ter FLIT). This is when you will perform your vault, so it's important that your afterflight is long, high, and graceful. A good afterflight depends on a good approach, takeoff, and repulsion from the horse. If these elements are executed well, the afterflight should also be successful.

Landing

Every vault should finish with a solid, well-balanced landing. Remember the landing is the last thing that the judges see, so it's important to make a good impression!

It's hard to achieve a balanced landing after a vault because your body is moving forward very quickly. This means that your upper body is continuing to move forward as your feet hit the floor. This can throw off your balance and cause you to stumble or even fall. To make up for this, you should land with your feet slightly in front of your center of gravity. As your upper body catches up with your feet, you will come to a solid standing position.

When landing, always come down with both legs slightly bent.

Notice how the feet are landing in front of the gymnast's center of balance.

The position of your legs will also help you achieve a successful landing. As you hit the landing mat, bend your knees slightly to absorb the force of your impact. Then quickly straighten your legs to give yourself a solid foundation and keep your balance. This is called "sticking the landing." If a gymnast does not stick the landing, he or she will have to take an extra step or hop. Although this happens often, it lowers the gymnast's score. One-tenth of a point is deducted for each step or hop.

★ COACH'S CORNER

A Landing Exercise

Just as you practiced takeoffs without actually performing a vault, you should also work on landings. One way to do this is to adjust the horse so that it is about waist-high. Place a thick landing mat in front of the horse. Then stand on the horse and practice jumping onto the mat. Concentrate on landing solidly on both feet without having to take any extra steps to keep your balance.

LET'S GET OVER IT!

Five basic vaults used in competition are discussed in this chapter. Each vault should start with a strong approach run. Move into your hurdle about three feet (1 m) before you reach the springboard. Drop your arms as you jump, and make sure your feet are in front of your hips as you hit the springboard. Then, continue as described in the following sections, depending on which vault you are attempting.

The Squat Vault

To do a squat vault:

1. Extend your body and reach for the horse as you leave the springboard.

2. As your hands touch the horse, lift your hips and bring your knees to your chest so that your feet clear the horse as you pass over it.

3. Push down and back on your hands to bring your body across the horse.

4. As your body moves across the horse, push up and away with your hands and block with your shoulders. Keep your legs in a **tuck** (TUK) position—knees and hips bent and drawn into your chest.

5. As soon as you have cleared the horse, quickly extend your body to a straight, vertical position and stretch your arms over your head.

6. Land by dropping solidly on the balls of your feet.

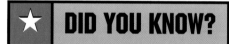

★ DID YOU KNOW?

Tumbling Moves

Many vaults use elements of tumbling, such as handstands, handsprings, and rolls. A good tumbling background will really come in handy as you learn new moves on the vault.

The squat vault

To perform a perfect squat vault, a gymnast must practice it over and over and listen to the coach for improvements.

The Straddle Vault

For the straddle vault:

1. Stretch your arms toward the horse as you leave the springboard.

2. As your shoulders swing forward over your hands, lift your seat and open your legs.

3. Push strongly with your hands as you pass over the horse. Your legs should straddle, or spread apart, over the vault.

4. After you pass over the horse, pull your legs together and straighten your body.

5. Keep your arms in front of your body as you land. Bend your knees slightly and recover to a standing position.

Keep your toes pointed down and out when performing a straddle vault.

The straddle vault

Speed and pushing hard with your hands results in a good launch.

The Flank Vault

   To perform the flank vault:

1. Swing your arms and upper body forward so that you are in an upright position as you land on the springboard.
2. Stretch your legs and lift your arms above your head.
3. Don't lean forward to reach the horse while you move through the air. Let the horse come to you.
4. As your hands touch the horse, bend at the hips and swing your legs to the side. Your weight should be balanced on both hands.
5. Continue by lifting your right hand. As your feet pass over the horse, bring your hips forward to align with your legs.
6. Push forward on your left hand while keeping your body straight.
7. Land directly in line with the springboard. Don't lean too far to either side as you land.

A good flank vault requires proper positioning of the support hand.

The Stoop Vault

1. As you leave the springboard, extend your body and reach for the horse to perform a stoop vault.

2. Lift your hips high by moving into a **pike** (PIK)—a position in which the legs are straight and the body is folded at the waist. Your hips should be above your head when your hands touch the horse.

3. As your hands touch the horse, whip your legs down. Rather than tucking under you, for this vault your legs should point straight down toward the horse.

4. Push yourself away from the horse with your hands. Swing your legs forward between your arms and let them propel you forward and over the horse.

5. As soon as you clear the horse, straighten your body and stretch your arms over your head.

6. Drop to a landing on the balls of your feet.

The stoop vault

More difficult vault routines, like the handspring vault, are easily
practiced on the safety of the floor.

The Handspring Vault

The handspring vault is more complicated than the vaults described on the preceding pages. You will want to learn it in steps. Practice with your coach to make sure that your body is in the correct position at each stage of the vault.

Before you start flying over the horse, practice by running and hitting the springboard. Then perform a quick handstand on mat stacks.

This handspring **drill** (DRIL) is used as a vault at the compulsory USA level 3. It will help you learn to extend your body while keeping it tight, and will also teach you how to block off the horse.

41

Once you have mastered the handspring on the ground, you are ready to move to the horse. Approach the springboard as described on page 29.

1. As you jump off the springboard, swing your arms forward and straighten your body as quickly as possible. As soon as your hands touch the horse, your body should be straight and ready to start moving into the handstand position.

A successful handspring vault requires the body to be straight and rigid throughout the routine. Then you bend your knees to cushion the landing.

When you attempt your first real handspring vault, you should have
plenty of padding around the vault for safety.

2. Move your shoulders forward as you reach the handstand position and push off the horse into a handspring.

3. As you leave the horse, bring your head forward so that you can see your landing position. You will land with your back to the horse.

This front handspring vault is expected for three out of ten levels of gymnastics. When you learn it with correct technique, your vaulting experience has just begun. Exciting and endless possibilities exist on the vault for the more advanced gymnasts. A handspring-full twist or double, or the handspring front tuck off in tuck, pike, or stretched position are just a few. Vaulting is over quickly, but its impression is a lasting one.

COACH'S CORNER

Naming Vaults

Did you know that vaults are usually given the name of the person who invented or perfected it? Many vaults are named after Japanese gymnasts, including the Tsukahara, which is seen often in gymnastics competitions.

One of the most recent vaults to be named after a gymnast is the Phelps, named after American gymnast Jaycie Phelps. A gymnast performing a Phelps will make a half-turn on the horse, followed by a half-turn into a flip off the horse.

GLOSSARY

afterflight (AF ter FLIT) — the part of a vault that carries the gymnast from the horse back to the floor

approach (uh PROCH) — a gymnast's run toward the horse

blocks (BLAHKS) — the act of pushing off from an apparatus

drills (DRILZ) — steps to learning any skill

handspring (HAND SPRING) — a gymnastic movement in which you spring forward or backward onto both hands, then flip all the way over to land on your feet

horse (HAWRS) — a piece of gymnastics equipment used in vaulting and other events

hurdle (HER dl) — the final step of the approach to the horse

pike (PIK) — a position in which the legs are straight and the body is folded at the waist

pivot (PIV ut) — to turn around a central point

pommel (PAHM ul) — the curved handles on top of a horse

preflight (PREE FLIT) — the part of a vault that carries the gymnast from the springboard to the horse

repulsion (reh PUL shun) — pushing away from something with great force

routine (roo TEEN) — a combination of moves displaying a full range of skills

GLOSSARY

springboard (SPRING bawrd) — a flexible board used to help a gymnast jump high in the air; also called a beatboard or Reuther board

straddle (STRAD ul) — a position in which the legs are held straight and apart across an apparatus

takeoff (TAYK AWF) — the action of jumping from the springboard toward the horse

tuck (TUK) — a position in which the knees and hips are bent and drawn into the chest

FURTHER READING

Find out more about vaulting from these helpful books, magazines, and information sites:

- Feeney, Rik. *Gymnastics: A Guide for Parents and Athletes.* Indianapolis: Masters Press, 1992.
- Gutman, Dan. *Gymnastics.* New York: Viking, 1996.
- Marks, Marjorie. *A Basic Guide to Gymnastics: An Official U.S. Olympic Committee Sports Series.* Glendale, CA: Griffin Publishing, 1998.
- Peszek, Luan. *The Gymnastics Almanac.* Los Angeles: Lowell House, 1998.
- *USA Gymnastics Safety Handbook.* Indianapolis: USA Gymnastics, 1998.

- *USA Gymnastics*—This magazines covers American competitions and athletes, as well as major competitions leading up to the Olympics.
- *Technique*—This publication is geared toward coaches and judges.
- *International Gymnast*—This magazine covers both American and international competitions and athletes.

- www.usa-gymnastics.org
  This is the official Website of USA Gymnastics, the national governing body for gymnastics in the United States.
- www.ngja.org
  National Gymnastics Judges Association, Inc.
- www.ngja.org
  This is the official Website for the National Gymnastics Judges Association, Inc.

INDEX

DATE DUE

GAYLORD			PRINTED IN U.S.A.